Dreams: Giants and Geniuses in the Making

Discovering the Power of Your Dream Life

Dreams: Giants and Geniuses in the Making

Discovering the Power of Your Dream Life

Herman H. Riffel

Destiny Image® Publishers, Inc.
P.O. Box 310
Shippensburg, PA 17257-0310

"Speaking to the Purposes of God
for this Generation
and for the Generations to Come"

ISBN 1-56043-171-7

For Worldwide Distribution
Printed in the U.S.A.

Destiny Image books are available through these fine distributors outside the United States:

Christian Growth, Inc.
Jalan Kilang-Timor, Singapore 0315

Omega Distributors
Ponsonby, Auckland, New Zealand

Rhema Ministries Trading
Randburg, Rep. of South Africa

Salvation Book Centre
Petaling, Jaya, Malaysia

Successful Christian Living
Capetown, Rep. of South Africa

Vine Christian Centre
Mid Glamorgan, Wales, United Kingdom

WA Buchanan Company
Geebung, Queensland, Australia

Word Alive
Niverville, Manitoba, Canada

Inside the U.S., call toll free to order:
1-800-722-6774
Or reach us on the Internet:
http://www.reapernet.com

Dedication

To our three "great" grandsons
Robert, *a Chemical Engineer*
Kirk, *a Skilled Craftsman*
Craig, *a Doctor of Chiropractic*

Contents

	Introduction	ix
Chapter 1	Giants and Geniuses	1
Chapter 2	From Where Do Dreams Come?	7
Chapter 3	The Road Maps to Life	15
Chapter 4	The Mirror of the Soul	23
Chapter 5	Dream Symbols	37
Chapter 6	Interpreting Symbols	47
Chapter 7	Animals in Our Dreams	51
Chapter 8	People in Our Dreams	63
Chapter 9	Dreams: Spiraling Stereogram	83
	Endnotes	93

Introduction

The greatest treasures are wrapped in mystery, whether they are in the form of an expanding universe with its quantum waves and black holes, or a life in a physical body that can be medicated and healed but not defined. So also is the mystery of language.

As J.R.R. Tolkien worked on the Elvish language for *The Hobbit* and *Lord of the Rings*, he realized that language presupposes a mythology. "In his view, language developed from a desire to relate experience, and not merely to convey information. To tell the past is history; but to explain the past, and to make it meaningful to the present, is mythology."[1] In the same way there is something mysterious about dreams. There is a picture to be shown, as well as a story to be told. Tolkien began writing, "In a hole in the ground lived a hobbit." It immediately became a picture that he wanted the reader to understand. Then he went on to explain the book that came out of the picture he saw. The classic story of *The Hobbit* that has resonated in the hearts of people the world over came out of that picture.[2]

Language, therefore, demands pictures and symbols, such as seen in dreams and visions. By that language the dream can speak of things beyond the dimensions of our time and space. It was this fact that allowed Einstein to dream of riding a sled till the speed of light threw the stars into fantastic colors, which led him to the theory of relativity. Therefore the language of dreams and visions is not limited to our three-dimensional world.

It is evident that Abraham Lincoln's Gettysburg Address went far beyond the rational mind, unlike the two-hour speech that came before his, and universally touched the deep unconscious mind of America with pictures and symbols.

The ancient Scriptures record the stories of little people who became great as they reached out to follow their dreams. Abraham, a nomad, believed his dream that told him he would be the founder of a nation, and it was accomplished.[3] Jacob, a wanderer, was kept from going too far astray through the remarkable dream of the ladder to Heaven. Joseph, a lad despised and hated by his brothers, a herdsman and a slave, nevertheless held on to his boyhood dream and ascended to a place next to the throne of Egypt. The ruler of that nation found direction through a dream that his slave, Joseph, interpreted. Solomon got his promise of unequaled wisdom, not through intensive studies, but through a conversation in a dream. Daniel could reach the monarch of Babylon, not because he had knowledge and understanding of all kinds of literature and learning, but because he was given understanding of dreams and visions.

Ezekiel broke through the realm of three dimensions with his description of the four wheels where each was "like a wheel intersecting a wheel,"[4] so that even today one of the scientists from NASA of the Kennedy Space Center in Florida is studying Ezekiel's vision, believing that somehow therein is a key to a law of the universe not yet discovered. Pilate, the Roman governor, was warned by his wife's dream about the danger of making a false judgment in the greatest trial of the ages. Peter, the head of the early Church, had to be instructed by a vision about his racial prejudice. John, the former fisherman, soared into heights beyond our sense of time in the things that he saw. Even Jesus spoke continually in the language of parables, which is also the language of the dream and vision. Unfortunately, much of the recent Church has missed it.

Chapter 1

Giants
and Geniuses

Come with me into the world of giants and geniuses, into the realm of dreams. That is where Einstein, Kekulé, Mendeljeff, and Niels Bohr were inspired to discover the theory of relativity, the molecular structure of benzine, the periodic table of elements, and the quantum theory. Even Bernard Mathias invented the superconductors in his sleep. It is the realm where Newton, Edison, Werner, and Goodyear received insights for their inventions, things that have affected the lives of millions.

For thousands of years dreams have given direction to world leaders. Alexander the Great was about to conquer Jerusalem when two dreams stopped him suddenly. *Alexander had a dream in which he saw the high priest in his robes.* That same night the high priest of that great city *had been told in his dream to put on his robes and meet the conqueror.* Therefore when the priest appeared in his robes, Alexander met him just as he had seen him in his dream and fell prostrate before him, to the consternation of his officers.[5]

Nothing could touch King Nebuchadnezzar, who built the magnificent city and empire of Babylon; he could elevate or execute men as he pleased. But two powerful dreams did what no man could do. They so humbled him that he bowed before the captive slave who interpreted his dream, to the saving of his life and empire. Constantine was directed to victory through a dream. Cicero chose his successor by the same means. Abraham Lincoln saw his death portrayed in most vivid dreams.

The Jewish nation owes its founding to Abraham's dream, and was later saved from famine by the dreams of Pharaoh, the king of Egypt. The church fathers Tertullian,

Synesius, Augustine, and many others pointed to the value of dreams. Rabbi Hisda in A.D. 200 is reported to have said, "An uninterpreted dream is like an unread letter."

Britain was saved from the destructive attacks of the German planes in 1940 through a revealing dream of a 29-year-old engineer working for the Bell Telephone Laboratories in New York. David B. Parkinson, the engineer, was working with a pen that scribbles voltage on a piece of paper, a device called a potentiometer, when he had the following dream:

He was in a gun pit with an anti-aircraft gun crew. There was a gun that hit an enemy plane with every shot. When he looked closer, he saw that mounted on the end of the gun was a potentiometer, just like the kind that he was using.

Upon awakening, he took the dream seriously and figured that if the potentiometer could control the pen, it could also control anti-aircraft guns. He took his idea to his supervisor, who eventually got it up to the Bell executives. Western Electric developed it as the M-9, which shot down 90 percent of the German V-1 planes that came over Dover. Parkinson was credited with turning the tide of battle in World War II by listening to his dream.

Ronald Reagan had repeated dreams of a white house. Thereupon the realtor showed him a big white house with bay windows that he felt he could afford. After Reagan became President and was in the real White House, he never had that dream again.

It is well known that Robert Louis Stevenson wrote the story, *Dr. Jekyl and Mr. Hyde* from a dream. Hippocrates and Galen, the founders of modern medicine, found great value for their work in dreams. Banting's discovery of insulin came in the same way.

The field of music has been profoundly influenced by dreams. Wagner composed *Die Meistersinger* in a dreamlike state, which was also true for Haydn and Mozart. It is said that Stravinsky's music was written through dreams.[6]

Dag Hammarskjöld said, "The more faithfully you listen to the voice within you the better you will hear what is sounding outside."[7] Ezra Gebremedhen, the former

General Secretary of the Lutheran church of Ethiopia, and later professor of Patristics at the Lutheran University in Uppsala, Sweden, spoke of the great value that the "church fathers" had placed upon dreams. Personally, he said, dreams had helped him in hunting and in improving his style of writing poetry.

Why do we need the dream to reach these heights? It is because the dream takes us beyond the three dimensions of the mind. Einstein could not discover the theory of relativity without going beyond our limited world. The rational mind cannot comprehend beyond its thoughts, but the dream leaps into a realm of insight to solve problems, to reveal new ideas that lead to inventions, to discover truths yet unknown, and to touch feelings that have been previously untouched.

Chapter 2

From Where Do Dreams Come?

If dreams are so meaningful, then from where do they arise? It is evident that they do not come from the rational mind, for the mind is often contrary to the dream, and limited in its concept. The dream goes way beyond the mind. Such was my dream as I related it to a friend in his home.

I dreamed I was in a greenhouse. A scientist and nurseryman raised a nutmeg plant and said that the previous year he had practically no calls for it. This year he had two hundred calls. Then I was told to raise many new and exotic plants for commercial use. The nutmeg plant had long green leaves with a spine and ribs going out from it.

Immediately my host got his encyclopedia, and without letting me look at the picture, said, "Please draw the leaf of the nutmeg tree as you saw it in your dream."

I drew it as I had seen it, and when he checked it he said, "It is exactly like the picture here in my encyclopedia."

To my knowledge I have never seen a nutmeg tree, nor do I have any recollection of seeing a picture of one. How did it come into my dream? That is a mystery! It never ceases to amaze me to find that dreams can reveal such surprising facts. We have cause to wonder how such knowledge comes into our dreams.

Dreams seem to relate to the things we are doing, to the problems we are worrying about. There is something uncanny the way dreams seem to come right out of the setting of our lives, and fit back into them like the right word in a crossword puzzle. The Designer of the universe evidently reveals His plans in the dream.

Sometimes a dream takes us back to childhood; sometimes it tells of present-day events with such reality that we think we are awake. Then at times it points ahead to the far distant future. In fact, there seems to be no dividing of time into past, present, and future as we know it in our three-dimensional world. In the dream it is all present. It is from our daily life situation, in which the dream finds its setting, that we find out to which "time" it belongs.

On September 6, 1995, I had the following dream: *I saw a cul-de-sac with a rather unkempt and deserted house that the French wanted to take into their deserted area, but the rest of the houses in the English area around it were well kept. The English wanted to include the deserted house into their domain, and finally succeeded in doing so.*

I had no idea what the dream meant. However, on the very day I arrived in Toronto I told the dream to my host. Immediately he said that it exactly fit into the Canadian political situation. The government of Quebec had just decided on a referendum to secede from the rest of Canada. Of course, Quebec is French and the rest of the country is English. I had no idea that such a thing was going on at the time, nor the meaning of my dream. But the setting was timed to our arrival in Canada.

Although I do not always know what the dream is saying, I know dreams are personal and relate to the setting of our lives. Since this was my dream, I knew it had something to say to me. It did not seem to relate to me symbolically, but to my surprise I found that it related specifically to the situation in which I found myself in Canada. On October 30, 1995, the referendum was held in Quebec province, and the vote was lost by those who wanted secession. So just as the dream had said, the "house" was restored to the English.

You may say that you do not have any dreams. But we now know that we all dream at least an hour per night. It is simply a question of remembering them. We forget them primarily because we in our Western culture have been trained to ignore them, for we have been told that dreams are insignificant and irrelevant. We must first be persuaded of their value before we give much attention to them. That usually happens when we have a dream, suddenly get an amazing understanding of it, and realize how accurately it has helped us concerning our problem.

We must recognize that the dream is like the furtive nocturnal bird, appearing and suddenly disappearing again before we can really get a hold of it. It must be caught before it escapes, before the day's activity stirs the mind, for the dream speaks when the mind is still. C.S. Lewis is reported to have said, "Wouldn't you be embarrassed if you were a dream walking around in daylight?" It is wise, then, to have a pen and pad with a little light handy to catch the dream immediately upon awakening, before the day's thoughts crowd it out. The radio alarm is most destructive to remembering dreams, for the announcer's voice catches our thoughts and so the dream vanishes.

Though I have been at the process of observing dreams for the past 30 years, I still have to do it with pen and pad handy as soon as the dreams appear, night or day. If I do not catch them in the first few seconds, the thoughts of the mind blow them away. How often I wish I could retrieve them, but they are gone. This is not true of all people;

some can remember their dreams more easily. Of course, if a person does not want to hear the inner voice, he can shut it out for a time. Only then it will probably break out in a nightmare that will dramatically awaken him!

Keeping a journal is an excellent way to record dreams, for they tend to come in a series. Thus one can follow the story over a long period of time. For instance, a man was shown his hesitations and progress in his dreams of a river. *At first he was on the shore looking at the river reluctantly. He stepped in a bit and then drew back. At times the river looked like a mad bull rushing down upon the meadow, and he was afraid of it. When things were a bit more peaceful he ventured out into the stream, but did not remain in it.* Finally, when he gave himself to the task to which he was called, *he saw himself in the middle of the great stream in his dream, and to his surprise he was enjoying it.*

We see the purpose of the dream in the experience of Nebuchadnezzar, the great monarch of Babylon. He was puzzled by his dream, but was so persuaded of its importance that he demanded an interpretation. When his astrologers and wise men could not interpret it, he ordered their execution. But a captive slave brought the king an answer. Daniel said that the reason this mystery was shown to him was "that thou mightest know the thoughts of thy heart."[8] The king's mind was filled with thoughts of his greatness and of the permanence of the kingdom he had built. But the thoughts of his heart came through the dream, saying that his kingdom would be wiped out, but he was more important than his kingdom. His kingdom would pass away and he would remain, so he better pay attention to himself.

The great purpose of a dream, therefore, is to show the thoughts of the heart over against the thoughts of the mind. All day we are occupied with the thoughts of our minds, which are important, but provide only half the answers to life. Dreams show us the other half, the wise, lasting, and great, creative "right brain" thoughts of the heart. They help us set our goals. They go beyond the three dimensions. They keep us in balance and make us whole.

A man from Canada sent me a letter saying he was tired of his job and had applied for a job with the Toronto Transit Commission but was turned down. Then he said, "That very night I dreamt that *I was in a room full of handicapped people with different disabilities, and they were all coming toward me. So vivid was the scene that every individual disability stood out. Feeling compassion for them, I took them in my arms and tried to comfort them—only I felt I was not good enough to be used.*"

Two weeks later he was hired by another company—to drive around handicapped people, just like the ones his dream had shown him! He loved those people and the new job proved to be the fulfillment for his life.

Chapter 3

The Road Maps to Life

Dreams are road maps leading to great destinations, showing the right way to follow, describing the dangers to avoid, and giving us helpful companions along the way. They are personal and private, only occasionally showing us what others are doing, and even then only in relationship to our own lives. Each person's map is personal and accurate. Nevertheless, the language that dreams use is symbolic, which is different from rational language, and so must be learned. It is an old language that we have unfortunately forgotten in our modern scientific civilization. But its value is so great that we cannot afford to take the road of life without it. Even the Bible universally uses dreams as divine direction.[9]

I paid no attention to dreams until the day I heard a lecture by Dr. Morton Kelsey telling us how important they were, but still I was too busy to do anything about it. Next year I heard another lecture on the same subject and decided that if there was anything to it, I would listen. That night I had an arresting dream.

I dreamed it was a beautiful day for mountain climbing, which is my delight. The sky was blue, and the sun had taken off the morning chill. My wife and three children and I had hiked beyond the tree line, well above the hill and forests below.

To the right of the trail, the mountain rose up sharply; to the left, the path dropped off toward the ravine. I was leading the way, my family right behind me: my wife, Lillie, a strong resourceful woman; Elaine, intelligent and charming; David, with his quick head for mathematics and love of detail; and Edward, blue-eyed and blond, our real nature lover.

The trail at the start was about three feet wide and covered with pebbles. It began to narrow

as it wound its way up and around the moun-
tainside. Finally the trail was so narrow that we
stopped. I saw we were in great danger, but
what could I do? Suddenly I felt the stones give
way under my feet, and with a shock, I realized
that all of us were going to slide and tumble
down into the chasm below.

Then I awoke. I was trembling. It was so
real to life. I had been in such dangers before in mountain climbing—the path crum-
bling beneath my feet, the deep chasm
below. It made me shudder to think of it. It
was a shocking dream, and I knew what it
meant. I could not get away from it. Since I
knew that the dream was speaking of my inner life, I knew it was saying that con-
sciously I was enjoying my life, climbing the
mountain with my family behind me. But
what about the unconscious?

I then learned that the dream often has
two parts, the present action, and that
which will happen if I keep going inwardly
in the direction I am heading. Therefore
this dream was warning me of danger before me. The resulting danger was pictured
in language that I could understand—
namely, the fall into the chasm—but the

meaning of it had to come out of the setting of my life.

Wherein was I leading my family into peril? Outwardly I was doing well, but inside my mind were strange thoughts. These thoughts would have been easily excusable to the world around me, but the dream made it clear to me that they would lead me into great trouble.[10] That was enough to awaken me to the truth, not only about this dream, but about all dreams. I must begin to heed their warnings and follow their direction.

That was 30 years ago. Now, after listening to many dreams and going through great trials as well as thrilling experiences, I am drawing into the last part of my life at 77 years of age. I should have retired long ago, but we were still traveling and lecturing when another vision came before me.

I see I am in a marsh, like wetlands, and before me is a series of mountain ridges, and beyond them lay a plain. Words came with the picture. They said, "You have one major work left to do. It will take you ten or fifteen years, and after that there will be time for writing."

18

The picture with the message surprised me, for visions are rare for me. Yet I knew I had not made it up. It was not the result of struggles and thoughts about the future with the conscious mind. It came out of sleep, unexpectedly, and yet so real.

Apparently the vision had caught hold of thoughts that had not yet come to mind, but already it was giving me an answer to questions not yet formulated. I could not dismiss it; I must wrestle with it and face the challenge. I knew it was not something that would automatically happen. I had something to do.

I know little about marshlands, for they were practically unknown to me in California. Still, I recognized that wading through water is not easy. This reminded me of the "muddy" situation in which I then was. The rest of the setting came out of what I loved to do. As boys my brothers and I climbed Mount Lassen, the 10,000-foot peak we could see from our home in the Sacramento valley of northern California. That climb was always a thrill and challenge in the summertime, when most of the snow had melted off the peak. Later, with others,

I had the opportunity to climb Mount Fuji of Japan, and Mount Egmont in New Zealand. But the highest peak I climbed was near the equator in Ecuador while I was chaplain to the staff of the radio and television station in Quito. I joined the young people to climb up Mount Pichincha, where we had to jump over the "death pass" and climb up to 16,600 feet above sea level. I knew that if I did not make the jump I would be dashed down into the chasm below. It was like the scene in the dream. Yet I love the mountains with their thrills and dangers. They have played an important part in my life, and so often come up in my dreams.

I knew that according to this vision I had waded through the waters. So when we arrived in Japan for seminars, I knew I had come to the end of the marsh. The mountain ridges I saw in the vision were steep and rugged. I know what it is to climb high ridges. They are not only challenging, leading to mountaintop experiences, but often the way down is more dangerous than the climb up. Between the high ridges are steep slopes going down and then up again. That was what I would face.

At that time I received a challenging task. I was invited to do a dream seminar/workshop for the prestigious Jung Society of Sydney, Australia. I was not a "Jungian," though I had studied briefly at the C.G. Jung Institute in Zurich, Switzerland. I had been a pastor for 25 years and since then had traveled as a lecturer, combining spiritual, psychological, and medical interests. Now I would have to face a large company of analysts, psychologists, and psychiatrists.

I chose to speak on "Individuation and the Spiritual Dynamics" to this Jungian body. It looked to me like a high mountain ridge to climb, and I was fearful of falling, though still greatly challenged by the opportunity. Fortunately I was able to make a good presentation, and when I did, I knew I had crossed the first ridge. Now I must go down to the valley below. How many ridges I had to cross I did not know, but the first part of the vision was fulfilled.

While in the valley between the high ridges in my dream, the setting reminded me of the high valley to which I had taken my bride 50 years ago. That was to the mining town of Holden among the Cascade

Mountains in the state of Washington, where we had 30 feet of snowfall that winter. The valley was so narrow and the mountains so high on either side that we could only see one third of the sky. Symbolically, for the past two years, we have been in such a valley, awaiting the climb up the next ridge.

So dreams are like a road map leading to destinations that are beyond us, warning us of dangers, but primarily challenging us to take the road.

Chapter 4

The Mirror
of the Soul

The language of the dream is different from the language of the mind. It is the language of the heart. The mind speaks in the language of thoughts and concepts, while dreams speak in the language of pictures and symbols. It goes beyond our three dimensions. For that reason we can picture Joseph's dream of the sun, moon, and 11 stars bowing down to his star, but we cannot put that picture, as we see it, on a flat canvas. There are things that we see in our dreams that we cannot describe. We can remember them clearly, but words and paint cannot depict them adequately. This picture language is our elementary language, the one we learned before we learned words and sentences. This language is unique to dreams and visions, but is not a part of our rational educational system.

For instance, *I dream I've gone over a cliff and am falling, but manage to grab a shrub and hang on.* The dream is saying that the dreamer has left solid ground and is falling. The dream pictures his thoughts or experience. The first part shows the present condition of the dreamer; the second shows what will happen if he keeps going that way. The first part warned him of the danger of falling, and the second told him how he can save himself. Since the dreamer was able to grab a shrub, it may picture a bit of growth in his life to which he is able to hold.

The questions that we may ask are, "How does that apply to me or my life? Am I thinking or doing something that seems good to me, but am unaware of danger ahead? What course of action am I taking that seems solid, but will lead me to a sudden fall?" The dream is not likely speaking of a physical fall, but rather of an emotional, spiritual, or even financial one.

The dream is like a mirror that reflects the condition of our soul or psyche. It is a good mirror, and its reflection reflects accurately. Sometimes its reflection is hard to follow, like the rearview mirror in a car as the vehicle drives around a corner, but it is still accurate. So our dreams accurately reflect the motions of our soul, though sometimes they are hard to follow.

An instructor in a college said, "I am an artist/teacher. Over the years I had a recurring dream about every three months. Although each dream was a little different, the feeling was the same. I am a potter by profession.

"In this dream I am searching for my kiln. I go out to school and discover that the kiln, which I had just fired, has disappeared. Someone has stolen it. The remainder of the dream involves a complicated and frustrating search. Inevitably I find the kiln, but in every instance, as I approach it, it is either collapsed, with walls and/or roof caved in, or terribly over-fired. In any case it seems that the work in it would be ruined. Then I look in the kiln and to my great joy and surprise, it is the most beautiful firing I have ever seen."

He went on to say, "I had this dream for eight years, but could never understand what it meant. One day, about a year after I had the last dream, I was reading a book. I hadn't even thought of the dream for a whole year. In the middle of a sentence, all at once, I *knew* the meaning of the dream. It was what some call an 'Aha!' Why it came at that point, I'll never know, but I *know* what the dream meant. I'd bet my life on it!

"This is the meaning: The kiln represented for me the 'creative process.' In my life as an artist, my primary desire is to 'create.' But as a man I have many roles to play that often conflict with my 'creative' time. I am a husband, father, teacher, and elder in my church. My dream was about this frustration. Everything else seemed to be 'stealing' my creative time, and as such it seemed to me that I was going to lose my creativity, or it would be ruined. But in the dream, when I did find the kiln, the work in it was stunning. This represented to me a promise from God, that if I took care of the other priorities in my life, He would see to it that in the end the products that I would create would surprise even me. I could now relax and stop worrying about the other parts of my life intruding into my creative life."

The instructor continued, "In my creativity class I had a young woman who felt she was very uncreative. One of the major assignments for the class was to do an end-of-term creativity project that was equivalent to a final exam. As the semester end approached, the young lady began to panic and even debated about dropping the class to avoid the project. On one evening I spoke on dreams and their relationship to creativity. The young girl commented that she had a recurring dream where she was trying to call her best friend, but she could never get through to her. I asked her what one thing her friend represented to her, and without hesitation she said, 'Oh, she's the most creative person I know!'

"The next week she came into class terribly excited. She had a 'eureka' experience during the week regarding her project and she brought in a truly 'creative' work. When she had finished with her animated presentation, as a final remark she said, 'And guess what? Last night I dreamed I was calling my girlfriend again, only this time she answered the phone. I finally got through to my creative side!' "

The same instructor told of another dream that led to amazing results in the dreamer's life. He said, "I had another young man, Bob, who also was in my creativity class. Bob was a surly young man who always sat in the corner and never said a word. He never handed in any work nor participated in class projects. Finally, I spoke on dreams in the class. I had mentioned that recurring dreams should be seriously heeded, since our unconscious mind was trying to tell us something that we hadn't yet resolved. In the course of the evening, I also spoke about some symbols that often have a universal characteristic. One in particular was water. I mentioned how at times water could represent the deep unconscious.

"At this Bob became quite animated. He told me he had a dream that occurred almost nightly. *In this dream he was in a boat on top of a large body of water. He wanted to jump in, but he was afraid there were terrible monsters in the water, so he didn't dare to venture too close.*

"Bob went on to explain a deep secret of his family. All the men in his family went insane by their mid 20's: his grandfather, his father, several uncles, and a brother. This gnawed at him continually. Although only 19 at the time, Bob wondered if he too would lose his sanity in his mid 20's. He was so frightened by the prospect that he refused to seek help from counselors or to share his fears with anyone. He didn't want to look in his psyche.

"So Bob pushed it out of his mind, or so he thought, and it in part caused much of his moody, anti-social behavior. He realized through our discussions that his dream was revealing his fear of his own unconscious mind. So he asked me what he should do the next time he had the dream.

"I told him to see if he could confront his fears by attempting to go into the water in his dreams, just to see what might happen. The next week Bob almost ran into class. He said he had to share something with the whole class. The night after we had talked, he had his recurring dream.

*"In the dream he remembered our conversation, so he thought he would 'test' the waters. So he sat on the edge of the boat and dangled his feet into the water, waiting for the monsters to arrive. They didn't! Next, he lowered himself in the water, but hung onto the boat. He watched closely, but still no monsters. Finally, overcoming his fears, he let go of the boat and drifted a short distance away. They came! At first they were just dark shapes below him. It seemed his dream was going to turn into a nightmare. But as he began to swim toward the boat, something wonderful happened. The shapes emerged out of the water and to his surprise they were not monsters at all, but dolphins, **friendly** dolphins, and all they wanted to do was play. For the rest of his dream Bob frolicked in the water with his new friends.*

"When he awoke his whole world seemed to have changed. His fears were gone. He *knew* he would not go insane. Life had finally begun for Bob. He never did hand anything in for the class and I had to flunk him. But on his teacher evaluation he wrote, 'I know I earned a failing grade, but that's OK. This has been the most important class I have ever taken, and although I

have failed academically, I have finally succeeded in my life, and I discovered I am not
a loser, but a winner. Thank you. Bob.' "

Once more the creative art teacher said,
"I had another dream that related strongly
to my art. I had reached a point in my work
as a potter where I felt I was no longer being creative. I felt I had arrived at a formula
that worked, but I was just repeating myself. I became so frustrated at not being
able to change directions that in due time I
began to stop working on my art. About
four months into this non-working period I
had a dream.

*"In the dream I was flying somewhere over
Europe. Next to me was an angel-type figure. As
I looked down I saw a town with many cathedrals. (I love Gothic cathedrals.) So I swooped
down and entered one of the buildings. As I entered the door, there was a large wooden mural.
I wanted to look at it later. So I entered the
main building. I have no remembrance of the
tour of the building, but I do remember coming
back to the room with the mural, only now the
room was full of Jewish worshippers, and I did
not want to intrude on their service. Disap-
pointed, I was led through a side door into an*

empty room. Out of the left corner of my eye I noticed a group of pottery vessels. So I walked over to examine them more closely. To my astonishment, they were all mine. (I could tell because I have a distinct style.) Yet I had never seen them before. They were **specific** *vessels and forms, and I can remember in my dream that I couldn't wait to wake up so I could draw them in my sketchbook.*

"In the morning I popped out of bed and ran downstairs to draw the vessels in my dream, for they were the *answer* to my creative dilemma. As soon as I opened the sketchbook and started drawing, the *specific* images were *gone*—simply gone! To this day I still have the page with a half-started drawing in my sketchbook. But what *did* remain was a feeling. First, the vessels had a great sense of *age*, as if dug up from an ancient ruin. Second, they were completely *three dimensional*. In other words, everywhere one looked there were things of interest. Up until then, my work had been meant to be viewed from only one side. Third, they were completely *mixed-media*, using wood, metal, rope, feathers, found objects, etc., along with the clay. That's all I could remember. But it was enough, since it opened up whole new possibilities that I had not considered before. Eighteen years later, I am still mining that quarry."[11]

It is easy to see that dreams are not simply pictures regarding our everyday life, though many are that. Rather, they speak very deeply to the heart and give creative directions for a lifetime. I was told that Mr. John D. Rockefeller was the first billionaire. He made a million a week in oil. He gave away money in dimes. It was by the time he was 33 that he was a millionaire.

At the age of 55 he became very ill with a serious disease. He lost all his hair and began to look like an old man. His stomach was so weak that all he could eat were crackers and milk. He ate those three times a day. Everyone knew he was going to die soon. In fact, a monument had already been prepared for him and a grave was ready to receive his body.

Then he had a dream. *He dreamed that when he died, he could not take any of his money along.* So he decided that he had better give it away while he was still alive. He started giving it away by the thousands, but a million came in every week from his oil business. So then he started giving away millions. He gave to large institutions, one of which was a medical institution in Peking, China, which was called the Rockefeller Medical Institution and Hospital Peking (now Beijing).

As he gave away his money, his health began to improve and he lived to 60, then 70, then 80, then 90, and at 97 he died! Mr. Rockefeller's dream showed him the value of his inner life, and as that was appreciated, the outer life prospered as well.

At times dreams show us something we are not willing to see. Our bedroom mirror accurately reflects our faces when we first awaken in the morning, but we may not like what we see. So our dream speaks to us, telling us that we need to make a few changes in our "face" before we go out to meet the world. But suppose that we do not want to make a change? The dream can say that we will "fail" if we go on as we are. The dream may not always be according to our liking, but it tells the truth, and following it will make us safe and keep us from failing.

Sometimes dreams are frustrating. *We are off to find our room or office, but we cannot find it. In the dream we look this way and that, and know so well where it is, but it is not there. We spend a long time looking and asking for help, but receive none.* In those times we must ask what our room or office represents to us. Does it represent our work, our position, or our place of escape? Inwardly, what are we trying to find? Have we lost our position among others and are trying to find it again? Or can we not find "our" work, though we may do our job for others well? Our soul is not at peace. Is the dream showing us that there is no place of escape?

The dream aims at bringing us into wholeness and balance—the balance of the heart with the thoughts of the mind; the inner life with the outer. We cannot be at peace until the two are unified.

How can we know whether the office in our dream speaks of our work, position, or escape? Which interpretation is correct? Here we come to the crux of dream interpretation. The dream comes from the dreamer, and only the dreamer will know the meaning of the dream. The meaning is taken from the dreamer's life. The interpretation does not come primarily from study, but from the experience of the dreamer. Dreams are most often subjective. Only the dreamer will know the setting of his or her inner life. Therefore the interpretation is not dependent on some rule or law, or upon some authority's knowledge. It comes from the dreamer. That is the safety of dream interpretation.[12]

As we begin to work with the dream, we may guess that the symbol of the office applies one way or another, but it does not quite fit. Then all of a sudden we know—we have the "Aha" moment—when we know how it applies to our lives. We have found the interpretation that "clicks." We know what the symbol means. No matter what others know about dreams or what their dreams are saying, the dream is ours and we know its meaning.

Chapter 5

Dream Symbols

The symbols of dreams are innumerable: the house, car, road, sea, sky, and anything that we can or cannot think of—even animals and people, as we shall see later. Your dream may pick up the television program, our teacher at school, the buttons on the dress, the horse that ran away, anything, and use it as a symbol or picture of something to illustrate for a purpose. Some symbols have common or almost universal meanings, but they are always subject to the dreamer's experience.

The house is common to all as a shelter, whether it be a mansion or a grass hut. The ocean often portrays the depth of the heart or the unconscious side of the dreamer.

The circle and the square are usually pictures of wholeness. Some animals have common meanings, such as the lion as king, the cock as the symbol of awakening, the fox of slyness, the snake in the grass with its subtlety, and the great devouring dragon. The eagle is pictured as the bird soaring high; then there is the dove of peace and the devouring vulture.

Nevertheless, each object must find its meaning from the dreamer. When we dream of our childhood house, it takes us back to the emotional, spiritual, or psychological house in which we lived as a child. It may remind us of the source of our present blessings, or of the healing that we still need.

A house under construction may show us the building that is going on in our inner lives. A house in a dream, even if it does not appear like the house in which we live, is still our house. We may discover that it has many rooms that we never knew were there. Such a dream shows us that we are finding out that our personality has more parts than we ever knew. We are growing, and there are more rooms of the heart to enter.

A friend from New Zealand told me this dream: "*I was in my grandmother's garden on a farm in Ireland. I looked at the farmhouse, and it had been beautifully whitewashed and painted and had lovely new lace curtains at the windows. I walked around the side of the house and looked into what I remembered to be the shop window, but now it was a big dining room with lots of tables with white cloths set with lovely silver. I then walked on to enter into the enclosed farmyard and it too had been all whitewashed and the hay barns were full of hay, overflowing in fact.*"

The woman then said, "Some time after having this dream, it came before me again and I wondered what it meant. The answer came as a clear word, 'It's all yours.' Again I wondered and the answer came again, 'It's all yours.' " She did not understand the message, so I asked, "What did your grandmother's farm mean to you?"

"Oh," she said, "it was the most wonderful place for me to go as a child. We children just loved to go to grandmother's farm. It was so beautiful and so much fun."

"Then," I said, "the dream is taking one of your most delightful memories and offering you something like it, even with improvements, but you must take it. That is, you must believe it is yours and anticipate it."

Now the word *whitewash* has a double meaning. Years ago, if the farmers did not have enough money to paint their barns, they would whitewash them. In other words, they would make them look like new. Today it has the idea of a coverup. So I needed to learn from the dreamer what whitewashing meant to her.

"Oh, that is making it all new!" she said.

If we were offered the gift of our best memory being made even better, we would be delighted. That is what the dream was offering her.

Sometimes, however, we cannot think of any symbolic meaning of the house that we see in the dream. Then we put that picture on the shelf of our minds until suddenly the association comes. We do not try to reason it out, but listen to our heart. Perhaps it is the house where we first met our partner, or where we signed a contract, or where we found shelter in a time of need.

Yet only the dreamer will know the meaning of that house.

The car is a cultural symbol. Although people everywhere have some kind of house or shelter, the car is particularly associated with the American culture, where it provides the primary means to get around. Therefore it may speak of our ego, our conscious self.

A girl of seventeen dreamed that she was driving her car furiously, even on two wheels around corners. I asked her if that was what her inner life was like. She agreed.

Occasionally the car may also symbolize our physical body. Remember, we cannot predict the meaning of a symbol until we find the association with it in our lives. The plane differs from the car primarily in that it takes us off the ground or earth. So it may picture our spiritual flights, or flights of imagination. If in the dream we are in a plane that is about to crash, we had better check our spiritual or imaginary flight. Soaring without a plane may more likely, though not always, be a picture of fantasy, or a desire to escape.

The ocean is deep, like our unconscious, and sometimes we find ourselves on the shore, afraid to enter. It contains many creatures, including fish that are good to eat. Those are good things we can draw out of the unconscious. But there also may be sharks, or memories that we fear are about to devour us. Above the waters of the sea are ships that carry us across the ocean depths; there we are safe in the ark provided for us.

The river serves as a good illustration of the many possible meanings to our symbols. To me the river is a place of adventure. I like to think of swimming and floating down the river like Tom Sawyer and Huckleberry Finn. To Lillie, my wife, the river is a symbol of death, for her brother and nephew drowned in a river. To some it may mean floods and destruction; to others it means life. To some it is water for the thirsty ground, and to some it is power. On the map rivers often serve as a boundary. When we cross a bridge over a river in a dream, it may mean we are entering a new land. Yet a river in a dream may have one of many meanings. Never accept just one possible meaning for a symbol. Take time to find the one that fits you in your setting.

Grass may picture new or fragile growth, as "grass on the housetops" at times. A tree may speak of stability and maturity, or the dark forest of foreboding. Yet the tree may also speak of fruit, or lumber to build a house. It may speak of the tree of life. We also know a tree once symbolized a great king overshadowing his land, providing for man and animals.[13]

Numbers all have their own meanings. For instance, one is the basic unit and may speak of our individuality. Two brings in a new idea. Three may be an integration of the two. Four is a common number of wholeness, as seven is the number of perfection, etc., but there are many other possible meanings.

Colors mean much to the artist, but have general meanings for all of us. We also can see how colors may have opposite meanings in different situations. Blue speaks of the expanse of the sky, though we may want to avoid Blue Monday. Green is a common picture of growth, but we do not like to associate it with being sick on the waves. Yellow is a sign of spring and new growth, but is also associated with the coward. Red has many meanings, such as anger, passion, love, Christmas, danger, blood, etc. We can see there is no end to the meaning of the many, many symbols in our dreams, but the richness of finding the right interpretation makes it very worthwhile.

The point of all this is that because there are many possible meanings to the symbols we see in the dream, the dreamer must find the meaning that speaks to his or her own situation. It can seem vague at first, but when we realize that the dream speaks out of and into the dreamer's life, then we understand that it is the dreamer who will know the meaning. You see this again and again in the dreams that are illustrated.

Some dreams seem utterly ridiculous, as did one of mine. Yet I am fully persuaded that all dreams are mirrors that show us something valuable. This was my "crazy dream": *I saw acres of dressed chickens, that is, cleaned and packaged, ready for shipment.*

I mulled over that for some time, and was not getting anything from it. There is such a temptation to ignore such dreams, but I have found them to be too valuable to discard. In fact, I would rather receive the little corrections from these dreams than wait until my situation becomes so serious that I have to have a nightmare to awaken me.

In this case I looked at the setting of my life. What was I doing? Then I had the "Aha" moment. I had just prepared a newsletter for my rather large mailing list, and I had determined to put something worthwhile into it. Suddenly I recognized what the dream was saying. By the special, spiritual message I had put into the letter, I had symbolically prepared the main dish of a chicken dinner for the many who were about to receive my letter. It was a simple encouragement to me.

Chapter 6

Interpreting Symbols

To help find the meaning of symbols, I play a little game with my audience by working on a dream that a little boy of ten told me. He said, *"I am tied to a railroad track and the train is coming."*

Though the dream is short and simple, the meaning of the symbols are profound. The first question I ask is, "What had the little boy done?"

There is silence for a time until someone ventures to say, "He must have done something wrong, for which he is punished."

"Does the dream say that?" I ask.

"No," they reply.

"Then do not imply anything that the dream does not say. This is very important, for we might infer many things, but we must stay with what the dream says."

Next I ask, "What is a railroad track?"

Here I may get an answer such as, "It is a path on which the train rides."

"Yes," I answer. "It provides a path, but what is it? How does it come about? Does it grow like a tree? Is it alive? Of what is it made?"

"It is made of steel."

"Is it just a chunk of steel?"

"No, it is steel that has been formed into a pattern on which the train can run."

"Can the boy change that pattern of steel?"

"No, that's impossible!"

"Good. How has that pattern of steel been formed?"

"It is man-made."

Then I ask, "Symbolically, to what is the boy tied, perhaps in school, that is man-made, and formed into a rigid pattern that he cannot possibly change?"

With a few guesses, they come to the conclusion that it may be a school curriculum to which the boy feels tied. The railroad track is man-made, therefore it cannot refer to the teacher, but the curriculum or course fits the symbol. It is rigid, and he cannot possibly change it.

Now let us ask the same question about the train. "What is a locomotive?"

"It is powerful," they say.

"Yes, it has power, but what is it? Talk to me as if I have just come from another planet."

Then they recognize what to do. "It is made of steel."

But again, "Is it just one piece of steel?"

"No, it is many parts of steel formed into a huge machine."

"Now, what does the locomotive represent symbolically that is like steel, has many parts, and is huge and powerful in the boy's school life?"

Finally they guess, "It is the test he is facing."

The test is man-made, of many parts, like a machine that looks to the little boy like a giant coming to destroy him.

This may seem like a long process, but these steps are necessary. After a while it is done quite unconsciously. We must first find out what the symbol is in the natural before we can interpret it symbolically. That understanding of the boy's dream would be so valuable to the parent, for the dream shows the boy's fears, though he may not want to verbally express it.

Chapter 7

Animals in Our Dreams

Animals provide some most interesting aspects to dreams. They frequently represent our emotions. It is worthwhile to study their habits to get the meaning they present to us symbolically. A young man presented me this dream:

"Our dog had died. Two of my brothers and I were carrying the dog to a place to bury it. We neither showed nor seemed to feel any emotion. We carried the dog down into a hole big enough to bury a large dump truck—very deep. Then we walked back out of the hole so we could bury the dog. We felt no emotion toward each other or the dog, and showed no emotion on our faces."

The man then said, "In our family we learned not to show our emotions, at least not the negative ones. Some of my emotions are buried deep. It is hard for me to let them out. It doesn't feel safe. It wasn't safe when I was a child."

On the other hand, when your dreams include huge animals, like the bull, elephant, or rhinoceros, that come charging head on, you can know that the emotions, like anger, jealousy, or lust, perhaps having been repressed before, are about to overrun you. You must recognize and begin to relate to those animals, to those emotions. As you begin to do so, the animals can change from the one charging head on, to the cat family, which attacks from behind.

At one time in my life I would be pursued by the lion, tiger, or others of the cat family in my dreams. Always I would run and hide to escape. Finally I learned about a valuable principle: "Always face your fear." So upon awakening, I faced the fear that the lion represented to me from the dream. Next night I found the lion became friendly in my dream. The last time I had a series of dreams with those animals, *I saw behind me, in my dream, a huge lion coming with leaps and bounds. I put out my elbow and the lion put his head through the crook of my arm and we walked off together.*

I had a powerful fear of expressing my emotions, which the lion represented. There is a lot of God-given energy in our emotions, like anger, lust, or jealousy, and it takes much energy to suppress them. However, that energy can be expressed positively or negatively. If we express anger negatively, it will be destructive. If we express it positively, by proper assertive action, it will be positive. So instead of suppressing the energy of my emotion, I began to allow it to express its positive aspects. The powerful energy of the lion became mine as I learned to integrate the positive part of the emotion that it represented. If we suppress that energy, which may be pictured in the dream as killing the lion, then that energy is apt to break out at the most inopportune time and in the most inappropriate way. So proper dream interpretation is really dream therapy, leading us to healing and wholeness.[14]

Horses often speak of power, as our language has indicated by the use of the word *horsepower*. It may be the libido energy, and is beautifully pictured in a dream of a woman, who told me, "*I see a whole herd of beautiful horses and am racing with them. They almost overrun me, but yet I am thrilled for the adventure.*"

From my journal I have this record: *I dream that a black horse is romping with me. I would sometimes be on its back, and it would roll over, but I would not be hurt.* It is a picture of the energy that I am experiencing in writing. It is wild energy; sometimes I am on top of it, and sometimes it rolls over me.

In our dreams we are often fearful of animals that are attacking us, but the dream has a positive purpose in mind. As Lillie and I were about to enter the Soviet Union while it was still closed, I was afraid and had the following dream:

I was in a little house which I knew was mine. A lion was trying to get into the front door, while a bear was watching the back one. I was afraid of both animals, but finally I let the lion in, and it took care of the bear.

I knew that the bear represented Russia. The lion represented the Lord of my life. That dream was telling me that I needed to let the lion enter my little house of fear. When we searched for the cause of our fear and let the lion come in, the fear was gone. That was pictured by another dream.

I saw huge elephants with their trunks raised come trumpeting toward me, but as they approached they fell and deflated like balloons.

All our fear of being interrogated and searched was gone and we went freely into the country. We were never interrogated nor our suitcases searched.

Dreams are practical and their suggestions invaluable. However, the principle that was suggested in the last chapter about becoming thoroughly acquainted with the symbol itself also applies to animals. What are their habits, strengths, and dangers? How do they apply to me in my life?

While I was in Zaire, Africa, the Sona Panga school director told me that *one of the boys dreamed that something terrible was going to happen within five minutes, and in less time than that a snake dropped from the roof on the bed.*

There is reason to fear snakes in Africa because of the many poisonous ones there. The dream was a proper warning for the boy and the class.

Snakes are in a special category as symbols. Because of the biblical story of the Garden of Eden, the snake has been known as a symbol of deception, and it often is that in the dream. Yet in psychology the snake is usually referred to as a symbol of wisdom. Medically it is a symbol of healing. therefore it is important that we do not interpret the dream based only on one symbol, instead of finding out which symbol applies in each case. One woman who is terrified of snakes dreamed this: "*I am surrounded by snakes, and I am not afraid of them, but know that I must be careful, for they can bite me.*" The snake in her dream could refer to a wisdom of which she is afraid, and can be painful to her, but which she needs to accept.

Such was the case with the Papua New Guinean woman whose husband dreamed *that all the fish he caught were dead.* That was interpreted wrongly to mean that all his children would be dead. She was known in that primitive village as the woman who would have no living children. When I heard about it from the women working there, four of her children had died in still birth or immediately after. However, we broke that fear and she had a beautiful child, as told in one of my previous books.[15]

Sometimes the animal's symbol is entirely unknown to us. If a person comes from the farm, the pig will often be associated with mud. Yet a young man from the city who wanted a pig for a pet, and had many pig figures in his house, told me how clean they were. He would interpret the pig differently from his dream: *I dreamed that the pig was with me in the kitchen and we were preparing dinner together. I loved it.* This was speaking of his pet emotion.

While reading a magazine I found a surprising use of the pig. The article said that in the days of sailing ships, pigs were used as an aid in navigation. When sailors were unsure of directions, they would throw the pig into the ocean, for it would always head north. When they landed, it was butchered for food. Thus the pig might be a symbol of helping us to find direction, or food.

A woman who was in the process of some inner growth and personality development dreamed this: "*I had been looking out the window at a forest in winter. About twenty feet in on the left side of the path was a tree whose branches hung over the path. Two owls were sitting on the same branch, one facing toward me, the other with his body forward but head turned to look at the other owl. I held my breath as I noticed that not only were there two owls, but about five or six feet back in a tree on the right side, on a branch overhanging the path, a little man was crouched. He looked like a leprechaun, except he was about one and one-half to two feet tall, the same as the owls, only much wider. He was dressed in dark clothes with a hat and had big pointed ears.*"

This dream was set in the forest, which may represent the mysterious, the area of the unconscious with which she was not yet acquainted. To this woman the owls represented something beautiful and free, which she rarely experienced. The leprechaun suggested the miniature form of her masculinity, small but with big ears. She reported to us that both the freedom of the owls and the masculinity needed to be integrated to fulfill her desire to help others through her garden work and her natural life.

Birds and insects are symbols in dreams as when the spider became a fearful sign of the enemy in Tolkien's *Lord of the Rings*. This was also true of a man in Australia, of what he experienced through his dream.

"*I was wandering about the grounds of the base. The grounds looked like they really were of the base; however, one corner looked a little like a part of the back of our old house. My children and some others were playing by the fence, which was made of plain and barbed wire, near a gateway with bush and trees on the other side of the fence. Where the children were playing was a small box with toys. I saw the box and was concerned that there might be Redbacks (spiders) in it, so I looked to see. I saw not Redbacks, but a large frog-green spider about ten to fifteen inches in size. I saw it come out of the box and catch a bird and carry it up to its web to kill and eat it. I sent the children away.*

"*I looked around and became aware that the web was over the whole field and was ten to twelve feet above the ground like a heavy net with thick, that is, an eighth of an inch, strands.*

This worried me, so I picked up a heavy stick to tear down the web and kill the spider.

"*As I began tearing down the side of the web, I was concerned, almost fearful of the spider falling on me. Even so, I continued. Then I saw the spider on the ground, but it was not the whole spider, just a few pieces of its legs. I thought, 'This cannot be,' but it was, and the bird it had captured was standing in the middle. It had lost nearly all the feathers off of its wings, but it had indeed killed the spider and eaten it, losing some feathers in the process.*"

This was a vivid picture of the spiritual battle going on in this man's work. The spider represented the evil force which, it seemed, was about to overtake him. The little bird, though, represented his own spiritual life, which had greater power than he realized. This told of the victory he could win, and gave him much encouragement.

A man said concerning his dream, "*I saw that my leg was very badly inflamed. In fact, I saw the red veins running down my leg. In the next scene I saw my briefcase, with a very poisonous spider sitting on it.*" It was a brief dream, but emotion-filled. Though the leg may have various associations, I asked him, "What do you use your leg for?"

When he said, "To walk," I asked, "Is there something wrong with your walk?"

Immediately he knew that I was referring to his inner walk, and he was suddenly aware of what the dream referred to. Then I asked, "For what do you use the briefcase?"

"In my profession," he said. So he knew that not only was he affected inwardly, but his outer walk was affected as well.

Two dreams together like this one, or two or three in the same night, often say the same thing in different ways. Apparently the spider had caused the inflammation of the leg, and it was now about to affect his work. The poisonous spider represented some evil of which he knew in his heart, but would not admit to in his mind.

At an important juncture in my own life I had a dream about *a big Canada goose in a debris-filled stream in front of a castle*.[16] The castle is the highest form of man's house; therefore, I was being taken to my highest potential. On the other hand, the stream that is filled with debris speaks of the river of memories from childhood. The goose is at home in the water, on the ground, or in the sky, speaking of my spiritual nature. Though there was a lot of cleaning up to do, the spiritual life near the castle was encouraging.

One of the greatest dreams I was ever told was of a lion. The dream was given to a man in his 80's in a retirement home in New Zealand.[17] It gave great hope to a man who, according to the general pattern of life, should have given up long ago.

Chapter 8

People in Our Dreams

Having people in our dreams is a very large subject that has been treated fully in my two previous books.[18] Most dreams of people are symbolic, but sometimes the dream is a literal encouragement to the dreamer. A woman whose childhood had been profoundly difficult had the following dream repeatedly in her childhood, when she was between the ages of 8 and 12 years. It was a great comfort to her, for she came from a home of great tension.

"I am in the narthex of our church, and I am climbing up the child steps for a drink at the

water fountain. As I bend to turn on the water and drink, someone turns it on for me. I look up into the beautiful face of Jesus, and His incredible eyes are full of love and acceptance. He smiles very calmly and gently."

Some dreams are almost literal, like the one from Mantua, Italy:

"A most learned young man, Hayyim Esperero, *dreamed that a Gentile high-ranking army man who had made life difficult for Jews was drowning in the Tiber River in Rome. In the dream, Hayyim Esperero rescued the man.* Hayyim subsequently informed the rabbi of Mantua of his dream and went to Rome, where he stood watch at the Tiber every day. On the thirty-third day, he saved a cardinal, who was a very important member of the curia, from drowning. This was a time when 216 Jews in Rome had been imprisoned because they were accused of killing a Christian child and using his blood. Because he rescued the cardinal, Hayyim Esperero managed to get the Jews freed and declared innocent of all charges. He was also handsomely rewarded by the cardinal, became wealthy, and was in a position of great help to the Jews."[19]

People in dreams are often misunderstood. But when we remember that the dream speaks primarily in symbolic language, we will understand that when we dream of people, we are dreaming of what the people represent. Misinterpretation of dreams and the hurt that brings most often come when we think that the dream is speaking about the one of whom we dream, instead of its symbolic meaning.

Dreams are parables, and some of the famous parables are like dreams. We tend to limit the characters of the parable to the people "out there" who do those things, but more deeply, they reflect the inner characters of our lives. The well-known parable of the prodigal son is not merely speaking of the prodigal who ran away from home, having received his inheritance; of the older brother who complained; and of the father who received them both and wanted to reconcile them. It is speaking of the prodigal in us, running

away from life. It is like the New York City
bus driver who, in the midwinter snows,
was found with his city bus in Florida!
There are times when we all feel like that.
The dream pictures the prodigal in us. It
also shows the well-disciplined but critical
older brother in us who has never recognized his freedom, but only worked like a
slave. The dream also reveals the reconcil-
ing father in us who condemns neither son,
but wants to accept them both.

How do people appear in dreams? Let
us begin with birth. Often women tell me
that they *dream of being pregnant,* but they
say that is not so. I say, "It is so, for you are
pregnant with a new idea or concept!"
Something new is being born within them.

*A woman dreamed that she saw a baby, but
did not know if it was hers or not. She then saw
a fetus lying on a hard cane chair, picked the fetus up, and it began to nurse and grow.* She
was seeing the new idea that she had just
picked up.[20]

At a critical juncture in my work, I had a
significant dream. *I was wheeling a baby carriage on a dead-end street. However, I drove the*

carriage up and over a house at the end of the street. It too was a new concept I had picked up, and I was shown that I had to overcome great difficulties, but that I could do so.[21]

Just about a month ago I had a dream that called my attention to a new project. *I am playing with our little baby, nuzzling my face against his, on a flat little bed. When I was beside the bed, the baby rolled off! Fortunately I caught him in my arms. Then I realized that we needed to put the baby in a crib for his protection.*

I did not know what the dream meant until the next day when I was visiting my publishing house. Suddenly I realized I needed to write another book on dreams, and the representative of the publisher immediately confirmed it. That was the beginning of this book. The dream was saying that I needed to care for that new idea. I had hardly given a conscious thought to writing this book, for I had another one in mind. But I was "nuzzling" the idea. The dream said that I needed to put the "baby" in a crib, or give it to the publisher, or the idea would fall away.

Sometimes we clothe our personality with a persona or mask to cover who we really are. Thus there are many symbolic meanings to the way we are dressed or not dressed in our dreams. Sometimes the dreams are quite embarrassing on the surface, but prove to be encouraging as we discover their meaning. A fine mother, but who had only a high school diploma, felt so inadequate when her son, Jimmy, who was studying psychology in college, would ask her questions related to his studies. Then she had the following dream: *"The doorbell rang and the newsboy was collecting. Jimmy called me to pay him and I came to the door stark naked! I awoke totally ashamed and embarrassed."*

The understanding came, however, when a friend told her, "You are to just be yourself, relax, and let Jimmy see and know you as you really are." "That helped me so much," she said. "The dream set me free. Jimmy and I now have a wonderful relationship."

People in dreams have many faces— faces that we put on:

"A man is never the same for long. He is continually changing. He seldom remains the same for even half an hour. We think if a man is called Ivan he is always Ivan. Nothing of the kind. Now he is Ivan, in another minute he is Peter, and a minute later he is Nicholas, Sergius, Matthew.... You will be astonished when you realize what a multitude of these Ivans and Nicholases live in one man. If you learn to observe them there is no need to go to cinema."[22]

A dream of a female artist revealed this: *"I am standing in the doorway of my home. Suddenly I realize I am expecting a large number of people for a dinner for which I am totally unprepared. There is no food in the house for them, and I knew about the event in advance, but find myself out of control in the situation. I proceed into my study and see people filing in for dinner. They sit at long tables and are patiently waiting for me to feed them. I go to the kitchen and find nothing. Returning to my studio, I look out from a balcony position and see the numbers increase from two hundred to three hundred fifty people. In an effort to get food, I go out to a local store for bread, but I am unable to procure it. Frustrated, I awaken."*

With great insight she went on to say, "First, all persons in my dream are parts of myself—the females are intuitive parts; the males are decision makers. My home is my being, and the studio is the creative aspect of my self. The long tables are my workplaces—altars, in effect. The balcony represents my effort to get a better perspective on the problem.

"Secondly, my dream tells me I am trying to solve too many concerns at once, to feed too many mouths on my own strength, all of which result in frustration. I need to find solitude, in which I draw my inspiration. Taking pen and paper I began to illustrate by drawing stick figures of the personal parts of me. I began to be aware of a great feeling of release within my being. By the time I had expressed all my thoughts, I experienced a total fullness."

When I dream of a man or woman, I need to ask myself these questions: Of what does that person remind me? What are his or her personality traits? What part of me does that person represent? Then I need to ask this: What is he or she doing that I am doing in real life? Dreams primarily speak about the dreamer; seldom about others. Therefore instead of thinking of the people of whom I dream, I am thinking of myself. The dream is there to help me, and heal and guide me. Other people are in the dreams to show me myself. That is what the artist saw in her dream.

A businessman had a dream about himself. "*I was going toward a playhouse when I felt a small tap on my shoulder. I turned around and found an Oriental man about my age standing behind me. He looked like a homeless man, but he did not give me a feeling of threat or fear. My initial feeling was one of annoyance because I wanted to get to the play. He told me he was asking me for any money I could spare. Initially I was not even considering giving him any money. But then I looked at him closer and noticed how he carried himself with a certain pride, along with humility. I could see that although he was homeless, he was taking care of his physical appearance as best he could. He told me about how he had worked in a kitchen and supported himself before he had an accident at work in which he was almost killed by a huge electrical shock. He had a long period of recovery and had lost his job and his apartment because he had no money left. As he was telling me his story, I was looking at his face, and he had this sort of smile that really looked like a smile of love. The more I looked at him, the more I felt his love and I quickly got a feeling of love for him. I decided to give him most of the cash in my wallet. He was writing out a receipt for me. As I was handing him the money I was locked on the loving glow on his face. I had a wonderful feeling as I awakened."*

Our friend, Tom, the dreamer, then explained the meaning he received from the dream. "The key to the dream is the homeless man. He represents me, that is, of my fear of not being able to provide for myself and my family. The loss of his job after having a huge electric shock represents my shock of losing my job five years ago. The loving glow in his face represents my love for the people both in my family and outside my family who helped me through that terrible time. The writing of the receipt speaks of my debt to these same people, which I hope to be able to pay someday. The love coming out of the homeless man also reminds me that I am learning to be a loving person." This served as a good and vivid reminder to Tom.

Dreams and visions are basically the same; the dream comes while we are asleep, and the vision breaks through our conscious thoughts while we are awake. However, we can't always sharply distinguish between the two. Both come from the deep unconscious, or the heart. An Episcopal priest tells of the dream or vision that gave her the guidance she needed to make a major move in her work.

"I was walking through the tunnel that I used each day on my way to the academic building. As I approached the end of the tunnel, I found that a waterfall flowed over the mouth. I stood in the refreshing downpour feeling renewed, and then stepped out into the sunshine. From where I stood, the ground sloped down gradually to a vast stretch of prairie. Wildflowers bobbed in the breeze, and I recognized the land as the area of the state where I owned a summer cottage. Then, just as instantly as the vision had come, it passed, and I was conscious again of the rough fibers of the Persian carpet of the room where I was."

She then said, "I had the vision and in less than two months we had moved. I had a wonderful job and my children have adjusted well and are at peace." The tunnel was the constriction she felt in her previous location. The wildflowers and stretch of prairie is what the land is like in the area to which she moved. The waterfall was the refreshing that she received in the anticipation of what the dream promised.

Sometimes the direction is partial; that is, it tells the dreamer to take the next step and then further guidance will be given. So it was with this man. "*I was finishing a meeting in the office of a local banker. When I got up to leave, he opened a double door to the office. The entire scene outside those doors was a huge body of crystal clear water. There was a pier or walkway that went from the door threshold out into the water. Pointing to the end of the pier, the man said, 'Go to the edge of the water and wait.'* " If he would follow the directions he was given and be willing to wait, he would get further guidance.

A voice in a dream is important. A teacher of social studies had the following dream. "*The setting of the dream was the hall-way of the school. My supervisor, a heavyset man, was talking to a young teacher, telling him what to do. No matter what the young teacher tried to say, the supervisor, a middle-aged, over-weight man, would silence him before he could finish a sentence and then remind the teacher what he was supposed to do and how to perform. The supervisor reminded the teacher to carry out the directives he had issued. The directives in-volved writing lesson plans for class and carry-ing them out according to the mandates of the superintendent. The young man tried to get in a word of response, but the supervisor would not listen. He just continued to quote directives and orders. Finally a voice from overhead say, 'Why don't you listen to the young man and his ideas?' And at that moment I awoke.*"

The teacher said, "I wondered why I had such a dream and thought of the unfair de-mands of the supervisor who restricted the freedom of the teacher to express himself. However, as I thought about the dream, I realized that the scene represented an in-ner dialogue within me. The supervisor represented my superego, the demands of society on my own impulses. I could not express myself as an individual who had something important to say. I had repressed my own originality of what should be done in my work of teaching. The dream pointed out that I myself, acting as the supervisor, was squelching my own creativity by referring to the demands of the supervisor who represented the collective unconscious of society within me. This dream made me aware of the internal psychic tensions between my spontaneous self and my internalized 'shoulds' of the social institution where I worked." It took a voice "from above" to awaken him to take heed of his inner tension.

John Gilmore was a civil engineer who graduated in the early 1950's. He had no computer training and was not able to get his company to computerize the work. Then he studied preliminary programming on his own and tried to write some simple programs. He kept running into problems with one of his formulas. Then came the help he had asked for, but not from the company.

"That night I had a dream. The correct formula was in my dream, and for the first time I

remembered the dream when I awoke. Two hours later when I was at work, I corrected the formula as I still remembered from my dream, and it worked. The formula had been @IF(AB>=1, "DE", "") and it didn't work. In the dream I was told to put a space between the last set of quotation marks, making the formula @IF(AB>=1, "DE"," "). This worked. Another time I was given a similar correction in the dream and it worked too." So whether the need is in the fields of science, literature, spiritual life, or whatever, the dream offers help.

Sometimes a wise old man or woman will appear to give "down-to-earth" helpful advice on a problem for which we have long worked. One woman dreamed this:

"I am standing in a small, lush valley, and on my right, coming over the crest of the hill, comes a figure. It seems he is a wise old sage–he looks and dresses like one of the shepherds of the nativity scene. He is somewhat stooped over from age and hard work. He is smiling and has a twinkle in his eye. He carries a staff, and at first glance I think it is the medical staff, but when I look again it is a stick with a roll of toilet paper stuck on top of it. Some of the toilet paper

has unrolled, forming a long ribbon that is blowing in the wind."

The dreamer said, "In the past I have taken my personal spiritual growth very seriously. Even though spiritual growth is serious, I can have fun. The shepherd has a twinkle in his eye. The staff in his hand is not poetic and profound, but practical. There is some waste in my life that I need to clean up and I have the toilet paper (wisdom) to do it. Personal growth can be fun and light-hearted. I can trust the (God-given) wisdom in myself to do what I need to do."

Sometimes there are dreams of the death of a loved one that can be very encouraging. The Episcopal priest said again, "In July I received word that my uncle was dying. That night I had a dream about him. *He was a younger man in my dream, more the way he looked when I was a child visiting at his house. I was out in the yard where he was working under the hood of his favorite red car. He saw me and smiled and said, 'Just trying to get this thing together.' Then he closed the hood and got behind the wheel and drove away...the car flew into the sky and was swallowed by a great light. I sensed love around me and felt joyful.*

"I told this dream to my older sister. She told me that my uncle had owned an early model of that kind of red car for years and he had always said that someday he was going to get it together." The dream gave an accurate picture of their uncle and then showed a symbolic picture of a blissful death.

A friend told me, "My cousin had many hardships come upon her. She had polio, which exacted quite a physical toll, and badly affected one arm. Smallpox left her face marked and drawn. Then she got a kind of disease that caused loss of control and consciousness, which resulted in accidents that left physical marks.

"One night in my dream my cousin appeared to me. She was the picture of health—a middle-aged woman of very fair appearance. No evidence of any marks or disfigurement were on her face; there was no evidence of anything but radiancy. She looked at me with a suggestion of a smile on her face. Then the picture faded. I remembered it well and still remember it.

Were I an artist, I could paint that portrait. Then I received a telegram saying that during the night my cousin had died." What a consolation!

Sometimes the dream gives warning so as to avoid danger, even death. So when a very heavy schedule was set up for me in Australia and New Zealand, I became totally exhausted. Then I had the following dreams in two successive days that gave me warning, resulting in my asking that one of my speaking engagements be canceled.

I went to a plane that landed. I talked to the pilot, but he could not answer. I soon found that he was in a coma.

In the second dream *I was on a lower floor of a hospital. A medical team of doctors and nurses came into the room where there were four elderly patients being sustained by life support. The team came with the decision to take the life support away. A nurse went to one bed and disconnected the life support from one man. He reacted by coming to and sitting up momentarily, whereupon I awakened.* That dream frightened me, and that, along with my exhaustion, caused me to make the decision to cancel an engagement. However, we are most thankful that for 25 years we have never missed an engagement because of illness.

I also had a delightful experience with another dream at a time where there was fear of death or serious injury. I was 67 years old and had never been whitewater rafting, though I grew up beside a river in California. This New Zealand river was rough, with number five rapids. The highest straight drop was 12 feet. Lillie was quite concerned about my going rafting. But the group that was formed consisted of a four-star general, a retired British colonel, and some other good friends, and I did not want to miss this opportunity. Thinking that she would be unable to dissuade me, she prayed that I be given a dream. *Fortunately, she had a dream, and it told her not to be afraid.* Of course, I had a good time. The dream is reliable, and if there had been danger for me, the dream would have told us so.

Chapter 9

Dreams: Spiraling Stereogram

A good friend, Dr. Bruce Morgan, who has combined the study of dreams and the spiritual realm with modern physics, says that scientists are excited about God and the new physics. He shows us how the dream can help us see through the world of matter and into the waves of quantum spirit. The new quantum science tells us that so-called dead matter is really alive and full of hidden patterns. Much like the modern stereographic craze, dreams pop out into an entirely new dimension to us. Dr. Morgan takes us into that land where we can learn to see the world in a new way through our dreams.[33]

Howard Rheingold wrote a Foreword to an excellent book entitled, *Stereograms*, in which he describes the human brain....

"as the most incredible virtual reality machine anyone has ever discovered....Every second of my waking hours, my brain converts a stream of perceptions from two visual detectors, two audio detectors, two position detectors, and myriad tactile detectors into the three dimension model I inhabit and call reality....I think we seek to create 3-D illusions in homage to the 3-D illusions our nervous systems weave. Learning to see the world in three dimensions is a natural product of our perceptual systems, but it is a learned skill."[23]

Just as we learn that skill, we can also learn to see the hidden patterns that come to us out of the fourth dimension through dreams. Dreams are the stereograms of the Spirit that can give us guidance, direction, and personal fulfillment.

Just as you learned to construct your present 3-D reality with your brain and physical senses, so you can learn to "pop out" new dimensions of the Spirit by using your spiritual senses.

Teilhard de Chardin, the great Jesuit paleontologist, coined the wonderful phrase, "spirit-matter." The songwriter was right: "The hills are alive with the sound of music…." Dead matter is alive and full of patterns. That is the genius of the new physics: quantum mechanics. Fred Alan Wolf, former professor of physics at San Diego State University, writes, "We might say that God's will is exercised in…the quantum wave function. It is a causal world of exact mathematical accuracy but there is no matter present. It is a world of paradox and utter confusion for human limited intelligence… Yet there is a pattern…a symmetry."[24]

So the net result is that there are patterns available for you and me in the invisible realm of Spirit. That is to say, our spirits have wonderful plans that can be implemented in a "causal world of exact mathematical accuracy." Pointedly, then, you can cause some good things to happen by resonating with God's symmetrical patterns that have been there eternally, just awaiting your interest and faith action and affirmation. You can follow your dreams to a more successful, happy, and fulfilled existence. Ralph Waldo Emerson wrote, "A higher law than that of our will regulates events...The whole course of things goes to teach us faith. We need only obey. There is guidance for each of us, and by lowly listening we shall hear the right word."[25]

Dreams are part of the energy of the universe, so when we have a question the answer is always there. It may, however, look like a confusing random dot stereogram until you relax your focus and learn how to look in the right way! Then the hidden patterns appear.

A friend separated for a time from his wife in a troubled marriage dreams of driving her back to their home in a sports car—but she is in the back seat criticizing his driving while he downshifts and enjoys taking the curves at high speed. Better not attempt reconciliation on your own terms. It won't work.

We would be perpetually dizzy and driven to distraction if we didn't have the marvelous dream that presents a hologram that we experience as 3-D reality. It is said that Cézanne, the father of modern impressionism, taught the world to see in a new way. That is what is needed here. We have spiritual eyes and ears—senses in our heart, or spirit, that can penetrate the invisible fourth-dimensional world and manifest hidden patterns, transforming them into reality in our daily lives. No wonder Einstein said, "Imagination is more important than knowledge."

I picked up a wonderful card that said, in part:

> "Youth is not a time of life, it is a state of mind, a temper of the will, a quality of the imagination, a vigor of the emotions, a predominance of courage over timidity, of the appetite of adventure over the love of ease. Nobody grows old by merely living a number of years. People grow old by deserting their ideals. Years wrinkle the skin, but to give up enthusiasm wrinkles the soul. Worry, doubt, self-distrust, fear and despair, these are

the long, long years that bow the forehead, and turn the growing spirit back to dust. Whether seventy or sixteen, there is in every being's heart the love of wonder, the sweet amazement at the stars, the starlight things and thoughts, the undaunted challenge of events, the childlike appetite for what next, and the joy of the game of life. You are as young as your self-confidence, as old as your doubt, as young as your faith, as old as your fear. As long as your heart receives messages of beauty, cheer, courage, grandeur, and power from the earth, from man, and from the infinite, so long you are young."[26]

I was lying on my back in an Alpine meadow and there, high above me, was this magnificent bird with stark white head and breast spiraling slowly in the thermals, its wings set in a modified "V" shape. I watched him in the binoculars until he became smaller and smaller and finally disappeared into the blue. That eagle did not learn to soar like that without getting kicked out of the nest, learning to flap those great wings, and crashing a number of times, but finally effortlessly being carried upward in the wind. We must follow the same pattern in our quest of dreams. We can learn.

Learn from the eagle. Journal your dreams and visions and then spiral around them again and again; a "centering" will take place. Carl Jung wrote:

> "The way to the goal seems chaotic and interminable at first, and only gradually do the signs increase that it is leading anywhere. The way is not straight but appears to go round in circles. More accurate knowledge has proved it to go in spirals! The dream motifs always return after certain intervals to definite forms whose characteristic is to define a center. As a matter of fact the whole process revolves about a central point or some arrangement around a center... dreams rotate or circumambulate round the center, drawing closer to it as the amplifications increase in distinctness and scope."[27]

Note Jung's terms: *chaotic and interminable – gradually – circles – spirals – revolving – circum- ambulate – rotate* — then the thermals. But the rewards are great. Patient inner work brings certainty and centering. Dreams can change your career, free you from slavery, and give you a new life. Spiral around them. Pay special attention to the chapter on "Circumambulation" in Dr. John Hitch- cock's excellent book, *The Web of the Uni- verse.* Here is a scientist with great spiritual insight.

When new patterns start popping out through dream work, it empowers us to change the world around us by means of the world within us. As Goethe said, "In this spiraling process, your faith and cer- tainty gradually grow into an inner know- ing and certainty." Remember Einstein said, "Imagination is more important than knowledge." Visualize, imagine, see as fin- ished what has been given you in dreams, visions, and intuitions. It will become so very real and certain that you will know, and those hidden patterns will be reso- nated into material manifestation. Dreams come true when stereograms "pop." Physicist Fred Alan Wolf described the process as "quiff-popping" when quantum waves of spirit reveal the hidden patterns. It's like a six-sided snowflake beautifully unfolding.

"With the wave aspect we discover patterning and dynamics which identify as spirit," writes Dr. John Hitchcock in another excellent book, *Atoms, Snowflakes and God*. He further states that concentration by means of meditation lowers the energy level of the body and gets it out of the way, bringing the mind to a point of calm.[28] "This is one means of increased perception of ripples from the patterning."[29]

Hitchcock writes, "When the 'aha' occurs in learning, it is as if something has fallen into place, and a new energy is released. It also seems as if the thing has been hovering around just out of reach waiting for an adjustment in the patterns of thought...."[30]

Conclusion

Let us then not limit ourselves to the three dimensions of our visual world, but dare to do as the prophet said: "I will stand at my watch and station myself on the ramparts; I will look to see what He will say to me, and what answer I am to give....[31] For God said, "When a prophet of the Lord is among you, I reveal Myself to him in visions, I speak to him in dreams."[32] With that attitude, we enter the realm of the giants and geniuses of the world.

Endnotes

1. Daniel Grotta-Kurska, *J.R.R. Tolkien, Architect of Middle Earth* (New York, Warner Books, 1976), p. 62.

2. Grotta-Kurska, *J.R.R. Tolkien*, p. 62.

3. See Genesis 12–50.

4. Ezekiel 1:16, King James Version.

5. Morton Kelsey, *God, Dreams and Revelation* (Minneapolis, Minnesota: Augsburg Fortress, 1991), p. 77.

6. R.A. Brown and R.G. Luckock, "Dreams, Daydreams and Discovery," a paper for The Polytechnic of North London Holloway, London, England.

7. Leif Sjoberg and W.H. Auden, *Dag Hammarskjöld Markings* (New York: Ballantine Books, 1964), p. 8.

8. Daniel 2:29-30, King James Version: "As for thee, O king, thy thoughts came into thy mind upon thy bed, what should come to pass hereafter: and He that revealeth secrets maketh known to thee what shall come to pass....that thou mightest know the thoughts of thy heart."

9. Herman Riffel, *Dream Interpretation: A Biblical Understanding* (Shippensburg, Pennsylvania: Destiny Image, 1993).

10. For more on my story of this dream, see my book, *Dreams: Wisdom Within* (Shippensburg, Pennsylvania: Destiny Image, 1990).

11. This teacher is Gary Wilson of Melbourne Community College, Melbourne, Florida.

12. For a more complete discussion on this topic, see Chapter 7 of my book, *Dream Interpretation*.

13. See Daniel 4.

14. Herman Riffel, "Spiritual Principles Involved in Psychological Counseling," audio and video series.

15. Riffel, *Dreams: Wisdom Within*, p. 113.

16. I talk more about this dream in my audio and video series, "Christian Dream Interpretation."

17. You can read about this dream in my book, *Dream Interpretation*.

18. See my books, *Dreams: Wisdom Within* and *Dream Interpretation*.

19. From the Hebrew book, *D'shaynim V'Raaanim*, as quoted by Monford Harris in *Studies in Jewish Dream Interpretation* (Northvale, New Jersey and London: Jason Aronson, Inc., 1994), pp. 94-95. Reprinted by permission of the publisher, Jason Aronson, Inc., Northvale, New Jersey.

20. Riffel, *Dream Interpretation*, p. 80.

21. Riffel, *Dreams: Wisdom Within*, p. 24.

22. Paul Meier, M.D. and Robert L. Wise, Ph.D., *The Ladder to Heaven, A Psychiatrist and a Minister Look at Dreams*, (Nashville, Tennessee: Harper and Row, 1995), pp. 60-61.

23. Seiji Horibuchi, ex. ed., *Stereograms* (San Francisco, California: Cadence Books, 1994), p. 6. Reprinted by permission of the publisher.

24. Fred Alan Wolfe, *Taking the Quantum Leap* (San Francisco, California: Harper and Row, SF, 1982), pp. 249-250.

25. Ralph Waldo Emerson, "Essay on Spiritual Law."

26. Anonymous. Taken from "Stay Young," issued by Klas Restaurant in Cicero, Illinois.

27. As quoted in John L. Hitchcock, *The Web of the Universe* (Mahwah, New Jersey: Paulist Press, 1991), p. 150.

28. John L. Hitchcock, *Atoms, Snowflakes and God* (Wheaton, Illinois: The Theosophical Publishing House, 1982), pp. 21, 157.

29. Hitchcock, *Atoms, Snowflakes and God*, pp. 164-165.

30. Hitchcock, *Atoms, Snowflakes and God*, pp. 164-165.

31. Habakkuk 2:1.

32. Numbers 12:6.

33. Chapter 9 is taken from the lectures and writings of Dr. Bruce Morgan. Dr. Morgan may be contacted at Box 3160, Cody, Wyoming 82414.

Order Form

Books

( ) *Learning to Hear God's Voice* ....$ 7.95
( ) *Dreams: Wisdom Within* $14.95
( ) *Christian Maturity and the Spirit's Power* ....$ 7.95
( ) *Dream Interpretation, A Biblical Understanding*......$ 8.95
( ) *Dreams: Giants and Geniuses in the Making* ....$ 5.99
    (New Release)

Video and Audiotape Series
Christian Dream Interpretation

( ) 22 half-hour videotape lectures, with manual $65.00
( ) 11 hours of audiotape lectures, with manual......$49.00
( ) Study manual.............................$ 6.95

Spiritual Principles Involved in Psychological Counseling

( ) 12 half-hour videotape lectures $45.00
( ) 6 hours of audiotapes $29.95
( ) Study manual.............................$ 4.95

Christian Maturity and the Spirit's Power

( ) 8 hours of audiotapes $35.00

Direct all orders and inquiries to:
Herman H. Riffel
2015 Stone Ridge Lane
Villanova, PA 19085

Phone: (610) 527-5389   FAX: (610) 527-1488

U.S. Postage and Handling (per item): Books $1.50; Tape Albums $3.00
Please include cost of postage and handling in your order payment–Thank you.

Name _____

Address _____

City, State, Zip _____

Prices Effective Through December 1996

IMAGE IS EVERYTHING
by Marvin Winans.

Yes, image IS everything! Does the image God has of you match the image you have of yourself? Society today suffers many social ills because of its lack of vision. Without an image we aimlessly grope about in life when we need to focus on what is true and accurate. We need the image that points us in the right direction—because *Image Is Everything*!

Hardbound, 204p.
ISBN 1-56043-262-4
(6" X 9") Retail $17.99

IS THERE A MAN IN THE HOUSE?
by Carlton Pearson.

With passion and eloquence Carlton Pearson calls to men in the Church to heed God's call to true biblical manhood. Our culture may be confused about man's role today, but God has never been confused—and His people shouldn't be either! This wealth of solid, Bible-based counsel will help you transform your relationships with both men and women!

CARLTON PEARSON

TPB-168p. ISBN 1-56043-270-5
Retail $8.99

Available at your local Christian bookstore

See all our exciting books on the Internet!
http://www.reapernet.com